THE LEGEND OF
UFOs

by Thomas Kingsley Troupe

illustrated by Francesca Dafne Vignaga

PICTURE WINDOW BOOKS
a capstone imprint

Thanks to our advisers for their expertise, research, and advice:

Elizabeth Tucker, Professor of English
Binghamton University
Binghamton, New York

Terry Flaherty, PhD, Professor of English
Minnesota State University, Mankato

Editor: Shelly Lyons
Designer: Heidi Thompson
Art Director: Nathan Gassman
Production Specialist: Danielle Ceminsky
The illustrations in this book were created digitally.

Picture Window Books
1710 Roe Crest Drive
North Mankato, MN 56003
www.capstonepub.com

All books published by Picture Window Books
are manufactured with paper containing at least
10 percent post-consumer waste.

Library of Congress Cataloging-in-Publication Data
Troupe, Thomas Kingsley.
  The legend of UFOs / by Thomas Kingsley Troupe ; illustrated
by Francesca Dafne Vignaga.
     p. cm. — (Legend has it)
  Includes index.
  ISBN 978-1-4048-6657-7 (library binding)
  1. Unidentified flying objects—Sightings and encounters—Juvenile
literature. I. Vignaga, Francesca Dafne, 1980- ill. II. Title.
  TL789.2.T76 2012
  001.942—dc23

                        2011025839

Printed in the United States of America in North Mankato, Minnesota.
102011   006405CGS12

TABLE of CONTENTS

THEY CAME FROM OUTER SPACE!

Suddenly the ground rumbles, and the sky explodes with
a burst of light. A strange object hovers above the horizon.
A UFO has come to visit!

UFO is short for Unidentified Flying
Object. Some people think these
mysterious crafts are from outer space.

People have noticed
strange objects in the sky
since ancient times.

In 329 BC Alexander the Great's journals describe a UFO sighting. Two gleaming silver shields in the sky spit fire at his army.

In more recent times, during the summer of 1947, an unidentified aircraft crashed near Roswell, New Mexico.

The U.S. military originally said they'd found a flying disc. Later officials reported that a weather balloon had fallen from the sky.

ROSWELL
CITY LIMITS
ELEV. 3570

To this day people still wonder if a UFO crashed near Roswell.

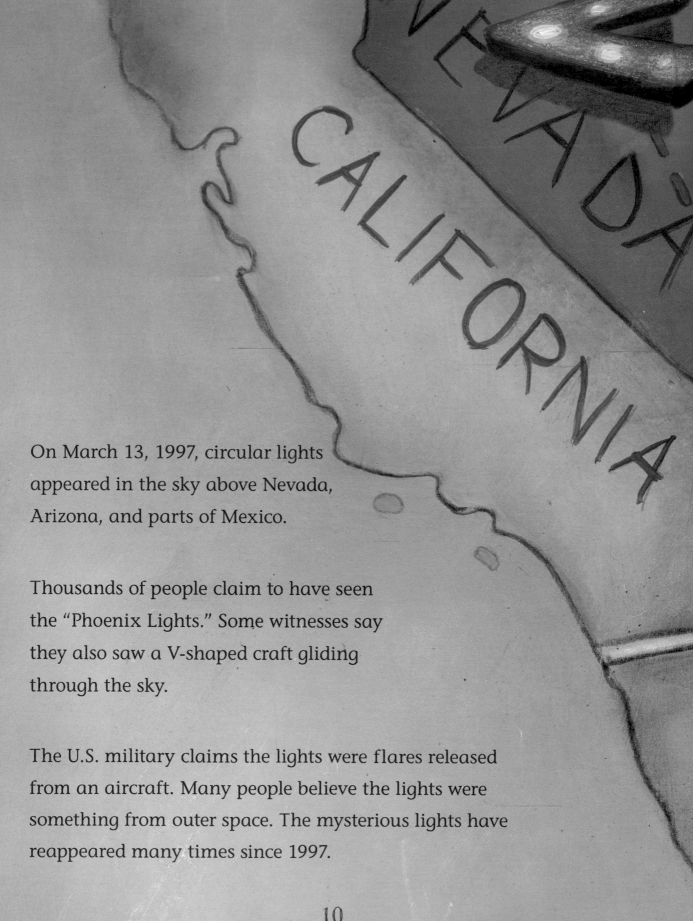

On March 13, 1997, circular lights appeared in the sky above Nevada, Arizona, and parts of Mexico.

Thousands of people claim to have seen the "Phoenix Lights." Some witnesses say they also saw a V-shaped craft gliding through the sky.

The U.S. military claims the lights were flares released from an aircraft. Many people believe the lights were something from outer space. The mysterious lights have reappeared many times since 1997.

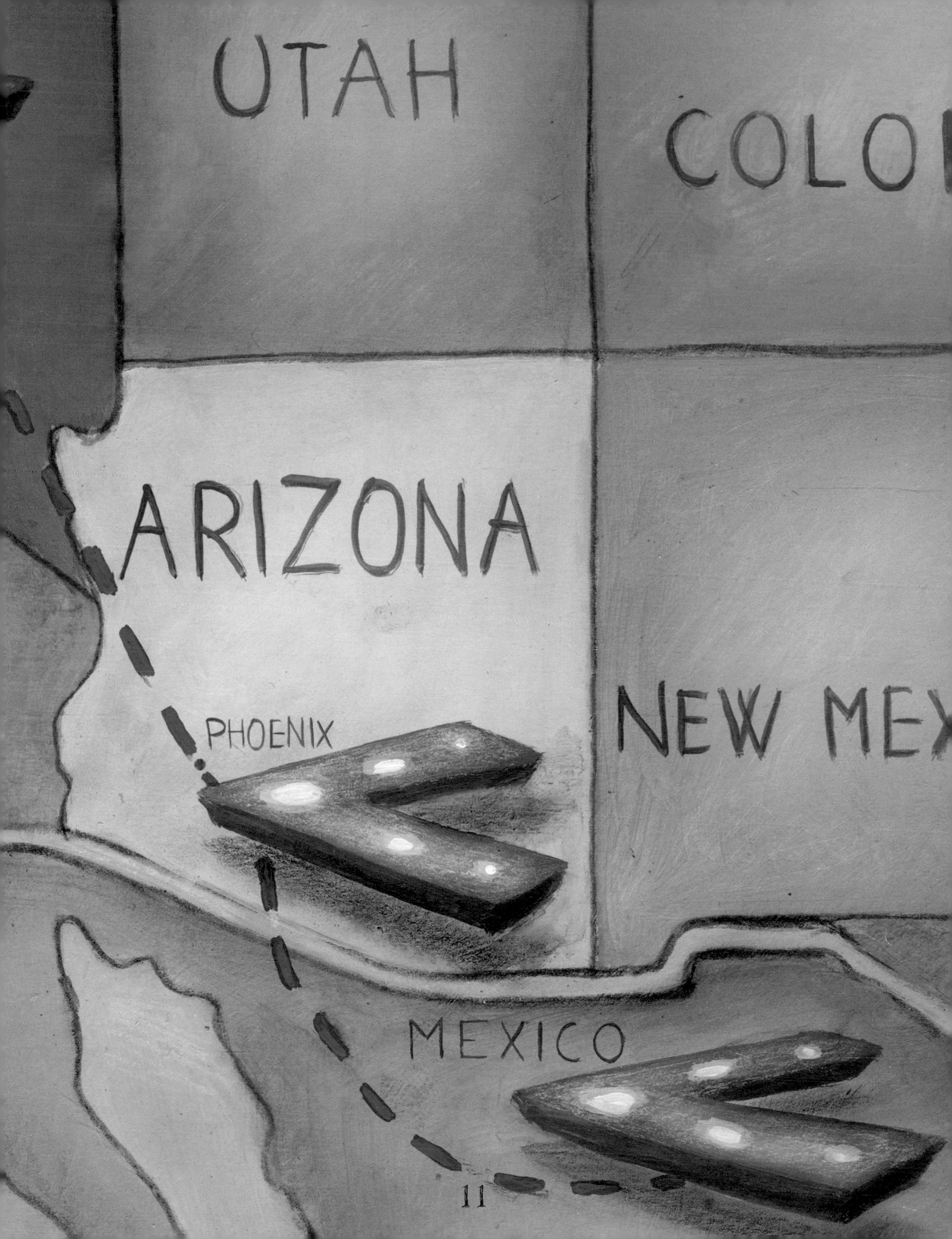
UTAH
COLO
ARIZONA
PHOENIX
NEW MEX
MEXICO

UFOS AROUND THE PLANET

On January 29, 1986, a glowing reddish ball was seen near Height 611, a mountain in Dalnegorsk, Russia.

Witnesses saw it rise and then fall a few times before it dropped like a rock. Two days later explorers found strange metal balls, splintered rocks, and burned trees at the site.

No other evidence
of a UFO was ever
found at the site.

Other mysterious
happenings around
the globe are crop
circles. Crop circles
are strange designs
made in fields.

Some people think UFOs make the designs.
Wiltshire, England, has had the most crop
circles, but the unexplained designs have
been found all around the world.

IDENTIFYING THE FLYING OBJECTS

One of the first UFO reports described a UFO that looked like a saucer skipping over water. Because of this description, UFOs are often called flying saucers. But not all UFOs are shaped like saucers. One UFO was shaped like a cigar and had smaller UFOs flying out of it. Some UFOs are round, with legs underneath like landing gear.

Others are shaped
like triangles.

Some UFOs are
said to have lights
around the edges.

Some UFOs don't look like flying saucers or spaceships at all.

People have reported seeing glowing balls of light in the sky. What looks like a shooting star may actually be a UFO.

UFO EXPLANATIONS

Not everyone believes UFOs exist.

Aircraft could be mistaken for UFOs.

A low-flying plane or a weather

balloon might look like something

from outer space.

Ultra-fast military jets and helicopters might look strange to us at first. Some people have claimed to see UFOs zigzag across the sky.

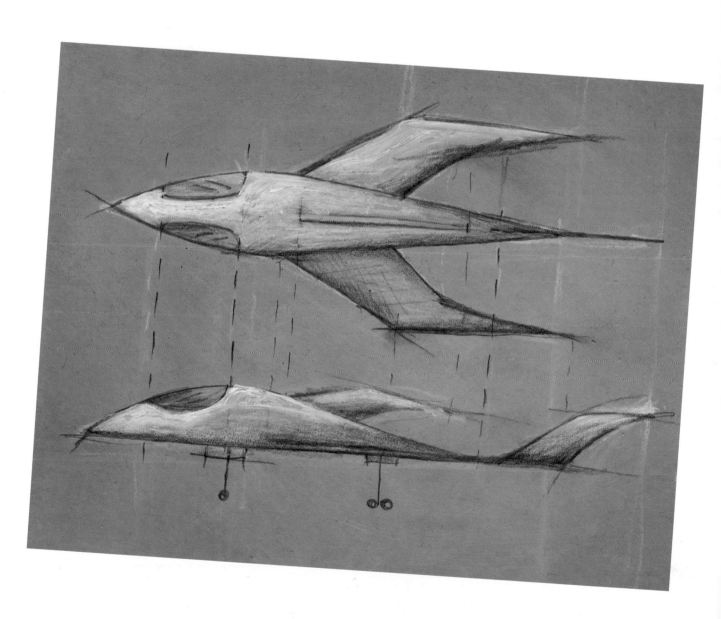

Could top-secret military vehicles change direction that quickly?

As UFO sightings became more common in the 1950s, some experts had a different idea. Psychologist Carl Jung believed people really want to see UFOs.

Many experts think simple things might look like UFOs to some people. Are their minds just playing tricks on them?

ARE THOSE UFOs?

Not everyone who claims he's seen a UFO is telling the truth. In fact, some people have created fake UFO sightings. These false reports are called hoaxes.

In 1967 brothers Dan and Grant Jaroslaw took a picture of a UFO. People believed it was real. Not even experts could tell it was fake. After nine years the Jaroslaws finally told the truth.

They had photographed a flying saucer model made from a Frisbee.

In 2007 a man filmed two UFOs soaring over palm trees in Haiti. The ships had many lights beneath them. As they flew off into the distance, a group of smaller ships seemed to join them.

Less than a month later, people were told the video was a fake. A man named Barzolff had made the video in less than a day.

We may never know whether or not UFOs are real. But many people still like to think they might exist. Look into the night sky or gaze into space. Was that a plane or a shooting star?

Could it be
a UFO?

GLOSSARY

evidence—information, items, and facts that help prove something to be true or false

flares—a burst of light shot from a gun

hoax—something made up, fake

psychologist—a person who studies human behavior and offers guidance

READ MORE

McNaughton, Colin. *The Aliens Are Coming!* Cambridge, Mass.: Candlewick Press, 2008.

Miller, Connie Colwell. *UFOs: The Unsolved Mystery.* Mysteries of Science. Mankato, Minn.: Capstone Press, 2009.

Rutkowski, Chris A. *The Big Book of UFOs.* Tonawanda, N.Y.: Dundurn Press, 2010.

INTERNET SITES

FactHound offers a safe, fun way to find Internet sites related to this book. All of the sites on FactHound have been researched by our staff.

Here's all you do:

Visit *www.facthound.com*

Type in this code: 9781404866577

Super-cool stuff! Check out projects, games and lots more at **www.capstonekids.com**

INDEX

THE LEGEND OF ATLANTIS

THE LEGEND OF BIGFOOT
by Thomas Kingsley Troupe   illustrated by Brian Caleb Dumm

THE LEGEND OF THE BERMUDA TRIANGLE
by Thomas Kingsley Troupe   illustrated by Carlos Aon

The Legend of the LOCH NESS MONSTER
by Thomas Kingsley Troupe   illustrated by DC Ice

Look for all the books in the
LEGEND HAS IT
series

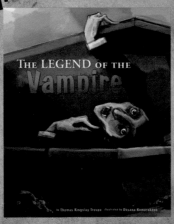

THE LEGEND OF UFOs

THE LEGEND OF THE Vampire
by Thomas Kingsley Troupe   illustrated by Oksana Kemarskaya

The Legend of the WEREWOLF
by Thomas Kingsley Troupe   illustrated by DC Ice

THE LEGEND OF THE ZOMBIE
written by Thomas Kingsley Troupe   illustrated by Francesca Rosie Vignaga